A Much Loved Toy Panda Bear.

Les McCloskey

Introduction

This is a short story about my life, my wife and child.
Why such a small thing like a cuddly toy could and did mean so much.

I hope it reminds some of you, of your happy time and your own cuddly toy.

A Much Loved Toy Panda Bear.

I don't remember when I got my little cuddly toy Panda bear. I only know he belonged to me, and I to him, yes he is a boy bear, I know this because he told me so many years ago when I was a lot younger.

    For more years than I care to remember my Panda became my best friend, I could tell him anything, Panda never got angry, or upset, he only listened, and my little Panda smiled at me all the time. He was always ready to cuddle and comfort me whenever I needed him, or when I was angry or upset. Panda was never judgemental. It didn't matter to Panda if I had been naughty or made a mess. He was always ready to climb into bed and snuggle up, listen to my troubles, and what I had been doing during the day before drifting off to sleep. I don't know how or why, but we lost touch for a long time. Years later, after I married, my wife found him tucked away in a box somewhere, holding him up for me to see, she asked if we would throw this out or send it to the charity shop. My heart skipped a beat the moment I saw him; memories came rushing back, I choked back a sob I was so pleased to see him. No please don't throw him out, I said Panda and I go way back, he was and still is, my best friend I told her.

My wife laughed, you big softy she said your to old to need a cuddly toy, I know. I said but reached out and took back my Panda. He felt so good to hold him, resting the Panda in the crook of my arm the way I had, all those years ago, it was as if we had never been apart, smiling down at the little Panda, I said hello my friend I have missed you. My wife laughing turned to walk away, you big baby, she said. Please don't listen to her I told Panda. She doesn't understand the connection between us. I suppose we must have been doing spring cleaning or something because lots of items resurfaced, old pictures, ornaments, pottery, pots, and pans. But Panda was very special, so he went into my pocket, with his head sticking out so that he could watch what was going on. The wife giggled every time she looked towards me and saw my Panda's head poking out of my pocket, I couldn't help myself, without realizing it, the wife caught me stoking Panda's head and looking at him lovingly. In the end, my wife said he means that much to you, does he? Yes, I said he does. We went through such a lot together as I grew up. I told her, I would hate to lose him again.

OK, she said, put him safe, and we will make sure we look after him, maybe when you're ready to let him go, you may like to pass him onto our child when we have one.

We were living in Leamington Spa, opposite the Warnford Hospital. When our son was born, it was 1st July though I won't tell you the year. I don't think my son would appreciate that. Anyway, the Hospital is no longer there; we had a first floor flat. That proved to be impractical, so we moved thanks to our landlord, who had another apartment just around the corner, he was such a nice man, it was much more extensive and on the ground level.

We stayed there for a few years while our son underwent Hospital treatment, It took a few years before we had a child, a baby boy, as it turned out. Unfortunately, he was born without a back passage; the doctor told us it hadn't developed properly and needed an operation to make him one. Also, his kidneys were underdeveloped, it was a devastating blow, and very worrying. Our Baby had other things wrong as well, but we were young ourselves and didn't understand all that the doctors were telling us. So my Panda took up residents alongside our baby boy. Pushing Panda into the cot and covering him up, I whispered to Panda, look after him the way you looked after me. Our Baby had

the first of many operations. At one day old, he had a kidney operation, at nine days the first colostomy. They brought his bowl out of his tummy so that he could function. Do his business in a bag, to give his little body time to grow large enough to undergo surgery to bring his back passage down and attach it to his bottom, and it took eighteen months for our child to grow large enough to have that operation. In the months that followed, our Baby had lots of dilatation (stretching the backside) until it was safe to close the colostomy. So that our son could use his bottom correctly for the first time, things went OK for a few months. Then he had a blockage, so they had to give our son a second colostomy lower down, and on the other side of his body, this one he kept for another couple of years, you can imagine the constant medication, day after day. We were living in Leamington Spa, opposite the Warnford Hospital. When our son was born, it was 1st July though I won't tell you the year. I don't think my son would appreciate that. Anyway, the Hospital is no longer there; we had a first floor flat. That proved to be impractical, so we moved thanks to our landlord, who had another apartment just around the corner, it was much more extensive and on the ground level. We stayed there for a few years while our son underwent Hospital treatment, a house came available in Warwick council-owned. We were lucky enough to get it and moved in. It was a three-bed house. We then bought the house under a government scheme, that gave council tenants the right to purchase, later I was able to extend the kitchen by ten feet, I had been in the building trade since I had left school. We got a grant that allowed us to have an extension to our bathroom above our kitchen so that our son could bathe easier it had a bidet and a toilet of his own.

We now had a two-bathroom three double bedroom property. I fitted patio doors. Off the living room, then we removed the wall between the room at the front and the living room, we then had a single room on the ground floor 23 feet long, I had a conservatory outside the patio doors leading to the rear garden. The front of the house was also 23 feet up to the pathway. So I removed the soil and laid a stone driveway, had the curbs lowered by now we owned two cars and could park them both on our drive.

My wife was a good mother. She kept our child scrupulously clean, and It was a continuous battle, with all the medicine, and hospital trips, Birmingham Children's Hospital. The doctors and nurses were fantastic. We would never be able to thank them enough. Our little boy's body was by now covered with scars from all the operations. We called these scars his maps so that he never developed a complex about them, to be honest, he had so many marks both back and front that his little body resembled a street map, but each operation helped save his life.

I haven't told you all that went on as our son grew up because some of it is so upsetting I think that I will leave it there. My wife, however, was very good at making things; she was an excellent seamstress.

My wife made our son fancy dress costumes so that he could take part in street parties. They were having at the time. All hand sewn. She had made so many dolls, her needlework was so delicate, so she made our son a cuddly toy clown it turned out very good (she called it corky the clown), and our son took to it straight away, replacing Panda, so Panda came back to me. Thanks, I whispered to Panda and put him away safe? As our son grew up, I suppose he got a little spoilt. I worked hard held down two. Jobs, so money wasn't tight, our son had everything he ever wanted, the best toys, he even had one of the first computers to play with, and computers were still in their infancy. But our son spent hours playing with it in his bedroom. I bought a kind of timeshare. In Portugal, a down payment of £5,000 it meant for five years we could go there any time of the year. For as long as we wanted. We had a choice of seventy apartments, at the cost of £68/week for a single residence. Or £99/week for a double one. Up to six people could comfortably stay in any of the smaller apartments. And up to eight people in a double. I took my wife and child there up to four times a year. Yes, I was earning good money.

Time has moved on, and years later, our son copes with his condition, though sadly, my wife, his mother, passed away over twenty years ago. She left a gap in our lives. It wasn't long after I lost her I had my first strokes, the first of many, that I am sorry to say finished my working life, I lived on my savings for a long time because by then, I had been self-employed for several years, no help from the govenment, but my wife left me with so many memories she had such a good sense of humor. I remember going on holiday to Portugal. I hired a car. The three of us drove along the coast to where we were staying, booked in, and settled down for the rest of the day, the next day, we planned to go out in the car.

Imagine my surprise, I got into the car and found Panda, sat in my hat wedged between the steering wheel and the windscreen, looking back at me, he had a small pair of sunglasses on and his big smile on his face. My wife had made him some
 shorts with a matching shirt and a little cap, a beach towel. She had found a small parasol and a little bottle of sun cream. She was so funny, and it must have taken her hours to make and sow clothing for Panda, I don't know how my wife had found such a small pair of sunglasses, giggling she said Panda needs a holiday as well doesn't he.

So Panda spent the rest of the holiday in my hat, we certainly saw the sites, we all came home with a tan, I never saw my wife sneak Panda into our suitcase, good job he didn't need a passport, I told her, I hadn't bought him a ticket ether? (funny girl isn't she).

Panda helping read the map

Panda eating Piri-Piri Sardines

Another time my brother stayed with us for a while, he would tease her relentlessly. He put his clothes out for washing. She washed and ironed them for him, then sewed all the cuffs up so that his arms could not go down the sleeves, and put them on his bed, my brother never found out until he was rushing to go out had to unpick the stitching in order to wear his shirt giggling all the time as he did so? They did get on well?

With all my wife had to cope with, I don't know how she managed to keep a sense of humor. Am I glad she did?

As our lad grew up, he had a lot of problems with schooling, because he needed changing throughout the day. The headmistress asked to see us along with our son's psychiatrist; we attended the headmistress went on to say how much, our son was a problem to the running of the school and that she and her staff did so much for our son, we should be grateful. **It got my back up having to listen to her go on.** The headmistress suggested he would be better off in a different school that they may be better able to take care of our son. I couldn't help myself. I spoke directly to the headmistress

I said, in a loud voice of course, we are incredibly grateful, and yes, we understand you do a lot for our child. Still, we can only hold a candle up to you for so long, if it were possible to remove our son so that he is no longer your problem we would. But for now, we can't thank you enough for all you and your staff are doing.

I saw the psychiatrist smile at that?

The headmistress backed down after that, she must have seen how it afected us, and we never had any repetition or problems from the school after that? Though I do know how difficult our son was. After all, we had him 24/7.

After my wife passing, I met another lady, she like my wife has a good sense of humor and we now live together, I get on very well with her family, they have two sons and a daughter, the oldest son, has a son. Her daughter has two children, a boy, and a girl, so we have three grandchildren. We love to see them whenever we can, but they are all grown up now and living there own lives.

During a visit to one of the son's who had started to foster, we met a child they had fostered, the child a boy, had a hard time at home his parents mistreated him, as foster parents, they had to limit physical contact with the child, no hugging without the boy's consent.

Anyway, we went to a wooded area with walkways and cycle tracks. They had brought bicycles along for the boys to ride, the foster child, lost control and smashed into a bush, he never cried or made a fuss, he doesn't show emotion? Something to do with the fathers control over the boy.

That night while putting the boy to bed, I went into his room and wished him good night, spent a moment or two talking to the boy, I asked him about his cuddly toy he was holding, he keeps me safe the boy said, I tell him all my secrets, he lets me talk to him. He's my best friend in the whole world.

It was all I could do to stop myself from crying for the child. It brought back memories from my childhood and Panda.

I choked back a lump in my throat as I said goodnight and closed the door, how people can mistreat a child is beyond me? I just wanted to hold the boy and tell him everything is OK, and he is safe.
I cannot describe that feeling, holding onto your best friend, crying, and telling him everything; everyone should have a cuddly toy to talk to and to cuddle, snuggle up to and hold.
(if that makes me a softy so be it)

I still love my Panda. Don't you wish deep down you had someone or something to confide in, I know it kept me sane. I'm over seventy now, but my memories of my Panda are every bit as vivid now as if it were yesterday, I know this is going to make some of you recall your cuddly toy or doll, that kind of childhood love you will never replace, it's so unique, isn't it? Even to this day Panda still sits on a chest of draws in my bedroom, (watching) I catch glimpses of Panda looking at me from time to time as I get dressed in the bedroom, each time I looked, he's still smiling at me, with that knowing look. He knew my innermost secretes, things I had told him and only him, but because Panda was my confidant, I never took him outside; instead, he waited for me on my pillow, ready to listen and hug me every night.

I had other toys that I could play with during the day, so Panda never came out. I have a loving mother, and though she had six children, my mother found time to cuddle and comfort me, she is in her nineties now. Unfortunately, my father used to drink and frequently came home worse for it.

I was told by family, that he would hit me around the head if I was close enough, though to be honest I have no memories of that ever happening, if it was true maybe I pushed it to the back of my mind,

I never cried when my father passed. (Sad that) we were never that close;

I do remember things from my childhood though things like, I was born in Birmingham, in 1948. I had a little toy animal that had a string around his neck, it could have been a dog lead of some kind, anyway I used to swing it around on the end of the dog lead,

I do remember letting it go, and it landed on a canopy above a door, that was the last I saw of it. I hadn't got Panda at that time, we lived at two back of one back of six Orchard Rd, and there was a tin factory just down the road.

We used to play in a school grounds close to it,

lots of miss shape bits thrown out into their rubbish skip, things like peashooters, functional but may have had a dent, so we used to salvage them.
Then buy a half penny bag of dried peas and play cowboys and Indians, shooting each other with peas, another thing we found was a spring-loaded gun. A single piece of spring wire bent to form the shape of a gun a handle and a trigger all in one, and a wooden bobbin pushed along the barrel against a spring, the trigger came up and captured the bobbin by pulling the trigger it released the bobbin. It shot along the wire barrel, and off the end of the gun, they hurt if you got hit, I could tell you. Both these items would not be allowed today, but it was fun for us kids back then. Kids can't even play conkers today.

We moved from Birmingham when I was six, to Warwick, to an area know as the Packmoors. I have fond memories growing up there. I, along with my siblings, we went to cotten end infant school.
Then moved as we got older to the attached junior school, I think maybe it was during those years I got my Panda, given to me to comfort me because you see I had ear infections that needed hospital treatment. For some reason, maybe because I was a small child, I was placed in a class a year below my age. The mistake rectified two years later when it was my turn to go up to the junior school.

Their remedy was to put me straight into the correct class for my age. Still, by then I was a year behind the rest of the form, my luck continued, you see before I moved to Oaken high school after my 11 plus, it was a joint education school for boys and girls, the year I joined they changed it, girls went to Beacham school attached. Still, next door, if you see what I mean, yes they separated us, boys went to Oaken and girls went to Beacham, and the year I left school, they changed it back to a mixed school, so I never got to learn about girls. I was eleven years old; I had moved to Oaken High School for boys when I had my first ear operation, which proved to be unsuccessful.

I had to have a second operation; they told me I would go deaf later in life, (I have, but not totally) without hearing aids I hear very little. Losing more education time after each operation,

I admit that I draw on my childhood memories when I write some of my books, what made me laugh then, hopefully, make kids laugh today?

Saturday morning, we used to go to the cinema close to the infant school, watch woody woodpecker, Roy Rodgers, Cowboys and Indians, and The Wooden Tops. All very tame by today's standards, but we loved it, and it gave our Mum a rest, times must have been hard with six children to look after.

I was one of three boys, the one in the middle, my older brother if he needed new trousers Mum somehow managed to find the money to get him a pair, same for my younger brother.

However, the worn-out pants did not go to waste; they got patched and repurposed, and I wore them, with large patches on my backside, thank heavens the girls could repurpose their clothes I may have grown up quite differently.

We group of kids got up to all kinds a mischief; we would set off bangers in the railway tunnel that ran from the lower part of the station to the upper because any noise down there, echoed, and the porter came running to find out what had happened. By that time, we were well hidden,

one of our group had picked up dog poop and put it in a newspaper, set it alight in the tunnel, and then set off the banger, hid as the porter came running.

Finding the paper alight started to stamp on it to put the fire out, then had to go and clean his shoes, naughty or what.

Behind our house, there was a black cinder path that overlooked a market garden. People that wanted vegetables or such would enter by a gate that had a small bell that would ring, alerting the gardener. He would come and serve them; the black cinder path was higher than the garden, we used to get small pebbles and throw them at the bell, making the gardener think he had a customer, he came quickly.

But, he found no one, by which time we were well hidden. He never found us out? Of-course I told all of this to my Panda because I knew he would keep it secret HEHE.
We lived quite close to the Hospital; they had an outside incinerator. I am happy to say it no longer exists.

But back then, we used to find old hyperthermic needles; we could smash the needle out of the syringe, and force the needle down a short privet stick to make a dart. Then fashion a set of flights tie them to the dart, and then throw them at the wash house door in the rear garden at the back of our house, a lot of these darts missed there aim and hit the wall.

The needle became blunt or bent, I threw mine it hit the door with a twang sound, I rushed forward to retrieve my dart, my brother threw his dart it hit me in the backside, I ran around screaming with the dart sticking out of my bum, chased by my mum. My brother rolling around on the floor laughing his head off, until Mum caught me and pulled the dart out. I told Panda that night I thought my brother did it deliberately?

I was thirteen and still wearing short trousers, the kids at school teased me, and I remember asking mum if she could let me have a long pair of pants because the kids are making fun of me at school, thank heavens she found the money somewhere? It must have been around that time I lost touch with Panda. (I was growing up I suppose) I can only imagine my mother would have put my Panda somewhere safe, knowing that Panda had sentimental value. How else could my wife have found him tucked away in a box years later,
Mum had seen how I used to cuddle Panda night after night, sometimes crying myself to sleep holding Panda? (Mum's are so sensitive at times, thank heavens)

I watched our child cuddling corky the clown and sleeping; in many ways, he had a happy upbringing, though he probably can't remember his cuddly toy clown. (Or maybe he doe's) He is a grown man now in his late forties, married, with two cats, no children though. All of those operations meant he would never have babies of his own sadly?

I consider myself fortunate I had a loving mother, a friendly Panda, and a loving wife, all of these have been the glue in my life, holding it all together.

Now years later, living with my new Lady, who also loves me, life has been good to me seeing me through all the bad times and the good. For those of you who still have there cuddly toy from there childhood, try this when you are alone pick up your cuddly toy and hold it the way you did when you were young, hug it and tell it you still love it, I bet you feel the love come flooding back to you because you put so much into it as you were growing up?

I just know you will feel much better for it. Take it from an older man who has found this very hard to share his inner feelings. Now I live with my Lady and our little dog in a bungalow. Fortunately, my Lady likes to grow flowers, so she looks after the garden flower bourders. I simply cut the grass, and I am now the proud owner of a brand new garden shed where I do my drawings for my books and a plack on the shed door that says Mr. Grumpy's work shop keep out. We also own a bird table, and as long as I keep filling the feeders, the birds keep coming. I love that watching the birds it makes me happy. Everything is rosy now. I think Panda's happy as well, and I think his smile is getting wider. Yes, I still have him?

Bye for now.

A MUCH LOVED TOY PANDA BEAR.

About The Author

Les Mccloskey.

Now in my seventies, I started to write books for kids as a hobby. I showed one to a friend who said why not try to publish it, so that's what I did. I have written and published five books so far.

Books By This Author

Mr. Mouse Needs A House.

Mr. Mouse meets a lady mouse, they want to marry but can't until he finds a house, some pages are left blank for children to draw in, or line drawing for coloring.

Skipping Through A Rainbow.

 Samantha. A Young Girl, accidentally skips through a rainbow, with magical effect, Animals start talking and helping each other and Samantha, Fairies, Goblins, Elves, and Imps. Fary Land.

Simon And His Geese Story.

At the beginning of the war, Simon Evacuated to Cumbria finds a Goose that had been shot, and he brings up her Goslings then trains them to a whistle the way you would a sheepdog.

Jane And Her Time Traveling Bracelet.

Janes Grandfather travels through time to give her a bracelet that lets her travel forward or backward in time to help relatives and family live better lives.

Mr. And Mrs. P. R. Ickles. Hedgehog Life.

A tongue in cheek look at Hedgehog life, how it could be. Or maybe it should be. Animals talk to each other, play together, and

live together. Even help each other.
Mr. and Mrs. P.R.Ickles. (Prickles)

Printed in Poland
by Amazon Fulfillment
Poland Sp. z o.o., Wrocław